Discard

# Habitats

# LIMESTONE CAVE

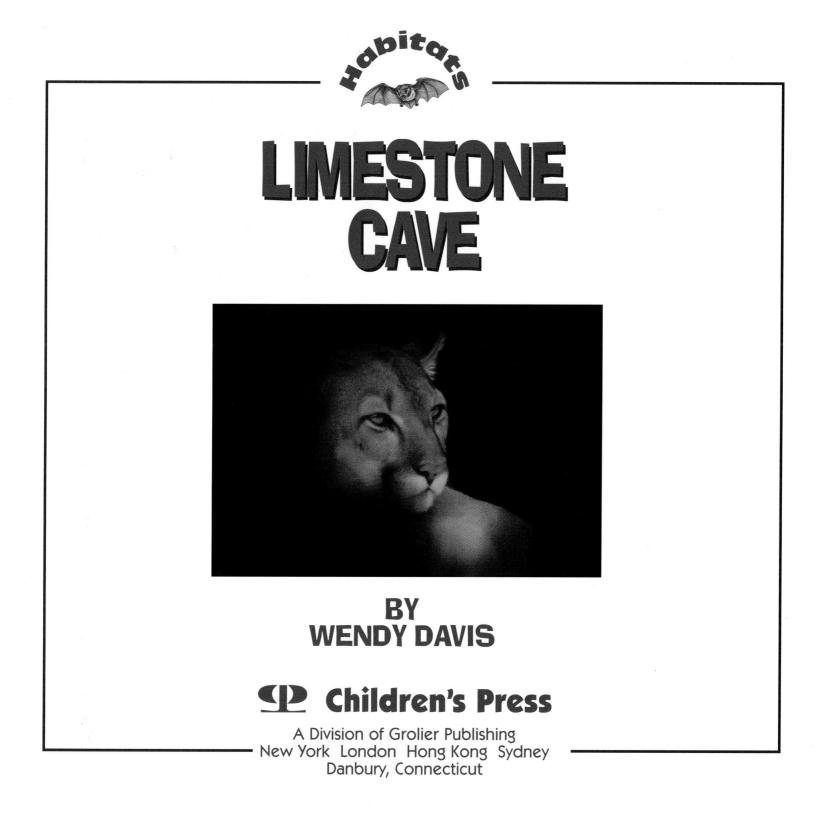

## BY
## WENDY DAVIS

**Children's Press**

A Division of Grolier Publishing
New York  London  Hong Kong  Sydney
Danbury, Connecticut

**Created and Developed by The Learning Source**

**Designed by Josh Simons**

**All illustrations by Arthur John L'Hommedieu**
**Photo Credits:** Terry Barner/Unicorn Stock
Photos: 3; Peter & Ann Bosted/Tom Stack &
Associates: 6 (right bottom), back cover; David
L. Brown: Tom Stack: 16, 24; John
Cancalosi/Tom Stack: 20; ChromoSohm/
Sohm-Dube/Unicorn: 4-5; Mary Clay/Tom
Stack: 14 (right); W. Perry Conway/Tom
Stack: front cover; David M. Dennis/Tom
Stack: 18, 19 (right), 26-27; Richard B.
Dippold/Unicorn: 19 (left); Dede Gilman/
Unicorn: 1, 12 (bottom); Kerry T. Givens
/Tom Stack: 21, 28; Russell R. Grundke /Unicorn: 11 (bottom); A. Gurmankin/
Unicorn: 11 (top); Victoria Hurst/Tom Stack: 14 (left); Joe McDonald/Tom Stack:
22-23; Mark Newman/Tom Stack: 29, 32; Brian Parker/Tom Stack: 6 (left); Frank
Pennington/Unicorn: 13; Rod Planck/Tom Stack: 12 (top); Robin Rudd/Unicorn:
10; Robert C. Simpson/ Tom Stack: 6 (right top); SuperStock, Inc.: 25; H. H.
Thomas/Unicorn: 15; Tess Young/Tom Stack: 17.

**Library of Congress Cataloging-in-Publication Data**
Davis, Wendy.
    Limestone cave / by Wendy Davis.
       p. cm. — (Habitats)
    Summary: Describes the habitat of the limestone cave and the animals that live there.
    ISBN 0-516-20742-3 (lib bdg.)        0-516-20371-1 (pbk.)
    1. Cave animals—Juvenile literature. 2. Cave ecology—Juvenile literature. [1. Cave Animals. 2. Cave
ecology. 3. Ecology.]
I. Title. II. Series: Habitats (Children's Press)
QL117.D38    1997
591.75'84—dc21                              97-26985    CIP
                                                      AC

Printed in the United States of America
1 2 3 4 5 6 7 8 9 10 R 06 05 04 03 02 01 00 99 98 97

Limestone caves are some of the most unusual and mysterious places on the earth. They are also among the oldest. Some, like this huge cavern, have been around for millions of years.

Caves can be found on all continents and in all types of terrain, or land. There are so many caves that cave explorers, who are called spelunkers (spi-LUNG-kers), often talk about a whole beautiful world beneath their feet.

Much of a cave's beauty comes from the action of water on limestone. As the years pass, water drips into the cave, dissolving part of the limestone rock. In its place the limestone leaves calcite, which often grows into stone icicles. Some grow down from the cave's roof. They are called stalactites (sta-LAK-tites). Others, called stalagmites (sta-LAG-mites), grow up from the floor.

Calcite creates other unusual cave formations, too. Draperies, popcorn, and pearls of calcite make caves into fascinating places to explore.

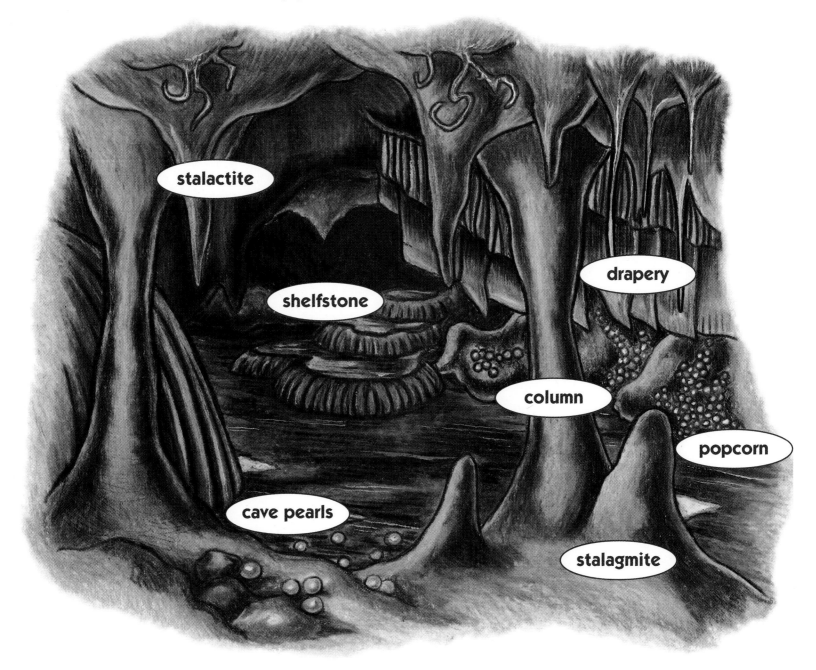

Caves are not just empty chambers of rock. They are also a habitat for many kinds of creatures. But, like cities and towns, larger caves are usually split into neighborhoods or zones.

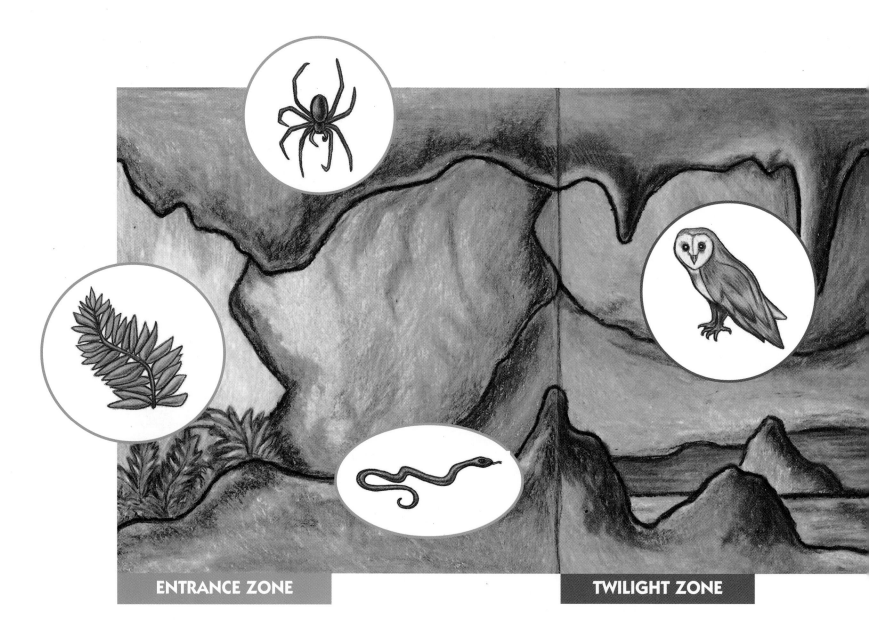

ENTRANCE ZONE

TWILIGHT ZONE

Just inside the entrance, for example, a cave is often light and breezy. This is called the **entrance zone**. Further inside is the **twilight zone**, where the light is dim but the entrance is still in sight. And way back, where there is no light, is the **dark zone**.

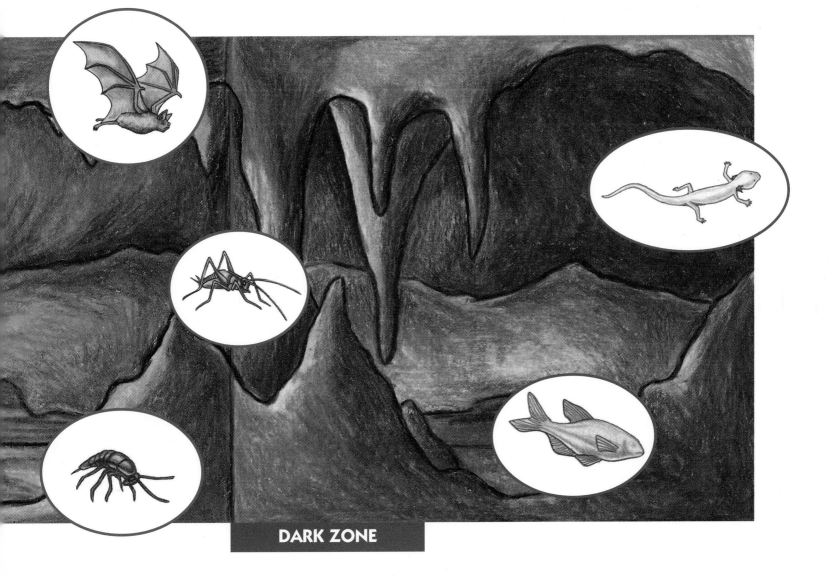

DARK ZONE

One very large cave lies on a hilltop in the middle of a forest. In the cave's bright, airy entrance zone, ferns and mosses grow on the ground and up onto the walls.

ENTRANCE ZONE

Daddy longlegs, spiders, and insects crawl back and forth through the entrance. Animals using this part of the cave are called trogloxenes (TROG-lo-zeens), or cave visitors. Most of them do not live here full time. They simply come and go as they please.

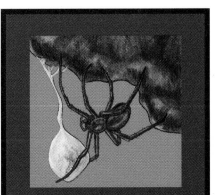

One type of cave spider protects its eggs by hanging them from the ceiling. Predators roaming the top of the cave often fail to notice the eggs as they dangle on a long, thin thread.

Some trogloxenes, like this little mouse, spend only part of each day in the cave. Others, such as this garter snake, may pass the whole winter here, protected from the weather. Inside, there is no snow or sleet and it is not hard to find a cozy corner for shelter.

A prickly porcupine uses this part of the cave as a den. The porcupine stays in the cave by day, then eats the bark of nearby trees at night.

A mother bobcat often hides her kitten in a nook of the entrance zone. Hopefully, the youngster will be safe there while its mother hunts for food.

At the very end of autumn, a female bear comes to the cave. She will sleep through most of the winter, waking only to go out for food or to give birth to a cub.

Farther back, deeper in the cave, the light grows dim. This is the twilight zone, home of the troglophiles (TROG-lo-files). Unlike the light-loving trogloxenes, these creatures tend to spend much of their time in the semi-darkness of the cave.

**TWILIGHT ZONE**

Owls often live within the twilight zone. Along with most troglophiles, owls sleep in the cave during the day and go out hunting at night.

Like people, owls can look at something with both eyes at once and tell how far away it is. Unlike people, owls cannot move their eyes in their sockets. That's why an owl must turn its head in order to watch a moving object.

A few troglophiles don't bother to go outside at all.
Many of these creatures are scavengers, which means
that they eat whatever dies in the cave. Salamanders
often get food in this way.

Certain snails, cockroaches, and cave crickets are scavengers as well. The cave provides these creatures with just about everything they need to survive.

Of all the troglophiles, none are more important or better known than bats. Once thought of as dirty and scary, bats are now considered among nature's most valuable creatures. In certain places, including parts of the United States, bats are even protected by law.

These flying mammals are well-suited to life in and around caves. Long claws make it easy for them to sleep hanging upside down. Bat wings are built for fast flying, while a bat's huge ears are perfect for picking up sounds both in and outside the cave.

Bats help people by eating large numbers of crop-destroying insects. In addition, bat droppings, or guano, make excellent fertilizer. In other parts of the world, some bats even pollinate the plants on which they feed.

Each night a bat will eat as much as half its own weight in mosquitoes or other insects. That's a huge amount for a creature that weighs only half an ounce!

A special system, called echolocation, allows bats to fly in the dark without crashing into anything. Although bats actually see quite well, with echolocation they can use sound waves to hunt for insects even in the darkest of nights.

The innermost part of the cave is the dark zone, where there is no light at all. This zone is so removed from the world outside that its temperature doesn't even change with the seasons or the time of day. Here is where the troglobites (TROG-lo-bites) live. They are the true cave dwellers—the ones that never ever go outside.

**DARK ZONE**

Most troglobites are blind. These grown cave fish, for example, do not even have eyes. But they are not sick or disabled in any way. They simply have no need to see in the pitch-black darkness. A troglobite's other senses—hearing, tasting, smelling, touching—are all very sharp.

Nearly all cave fish are born with eyes. But as the fish grow up, their eyes get smaller and smaller. Soon a layer of skin forms over the eyes, and eventually they are completely hidden.

This salamander is colorless. Again, there is nothing wrong. It simply lives in total darkness and doesn't need skin color for protection from the sun. The skin coverings of many troglobites are sometimes so thin that you can see right through them.

In time, species often become better suited to their habitats. This is called adaptation. (A species is a specific group of living things such as little brown bats or black bears or even humans.)

Adaptation is complicated and takes a long time. Troglobites have become especially adapted to life deep in caves, so much so that they cannot live anywhere else.

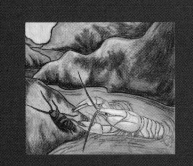

In all caves, the food chain starts outside. Animal visitors and underground streams bring in food in the form of dead animals, insects, and droppings. Bigger troglobites often eat smaller ones whose food has come from the outside world.

Troglobites are small and do not need much food. This crayfish does quite well scavenging for whatever it can find. Long feelers help with the search.

Outside, day turns to night, and the seasons come and go. But deep inside the cave there is only dim light or darkness. Still, as long as animals use it for shelter—and as long as water keeps seeping in—the strange, fascinating life of the cave will continue.

# More About

**Spider, page 11:**
Although most spiders have eight eyes, some types have two, four, or even six. Certain cave spiders have no eyes at all.

**Porcupine, page 13:**
Despite what some may say, porcupines don't shoot quills at their enemies. When a porcupine hits something with its tail, the tail's hooked quills come out and often stay in the victim's flesh.

**Mouse, page 12:**
White-footed mice, or deer mice, often build nests in cracks between cave rocks. As soon as the nests become dirty, the mice make new ones.

**Bobcat, page 14:**
Though small, a bobcat is fierce and strong enough to leap onto the back of a young deer and kill it.

**Garter snake, page 12:**
Most snakes lay eggs. But garter snakes give birth to live young. The average size of a litter of baby garter snakes is 18.

**Great Horned Owl, page 17:**
The great horned owl is about 2 feet (61 centimeters) long. Its call—whoo, hoo-hoo, whoo, whoo—can sound like a dog barking in the distance.

# This Habitat

**Snail, page 19:**
When a snail moves, it pours out a sticky liquid called mucus. This makes a path that helps the animal slide along. It also protects the snail from sharp objects.

**Blind Cave Fish, page 25:**
There is a row of sense organs along each side of a cave fish's body. These organs pick up the smallest vibrations and help the fish feel its way around.

**Cave Cricket, page 19:**
A cave cricket has extra long antennae that can sense danger a long way off. This gives the cricket plenty of time to leap to safety.

**Cave Salamander, pages 26-27:**
Most states have a state flower or a state bird. But Tennessee even has a state amphibian. It is the cave salamander, a creature that is found in streams in the many limestone caves of Tennessee.

**Bat, page 21:**
Most bats have only one baby per year. The young bat usually clings to its mother for three weeks before it is ready to fly off on its own.

**Crayfish, page 28:**
The outside of a crayfish has a hard shell called the exoskeleton. It acts like a suit of armor, protecting the crayfish's soft body parts from injury.